25 Super-Fun Spelling Games

by Nancy Jolson Leber

SCHOLASTIC
PROFESSIONAL **B**OOKS

NEW YORK · TORONTO · LONDON · AUCKLAND · SYDNEY
MEXICO CITY · NEW DELHI · HONG KONG

ACKNOWLEDGMENTS
*I would like to express my thanks to my colleagues—
Alice Dickstein for introducing me to this project, Gail Tuchman for her spelling
leadership and enthusiasm, and Amy Levin for her partnership.*

*My gratitude also goes to editors Liza Charlesworth and Danielle Blood
for their professionalism.*

DEDICATION
*I would like to dedicate this book to my favorite teacher—
Dr. Marvin A. Jolson, my father.*

Cover design by Pamela Simmons
Interior design by Solutions by Design, Inc.
Cover and interior illustrations by Rick Stromoski

ISBN 0-590-52211-6
Copyright ©1999 by Nancy Jolson Leber
All rights reserved. Printed in the U.S.A.

Contents

Reproducibles

Word Lists

Practice Tests

Game Sign-Out Sheet

Professional Bibliography

Introduction

It happens all the time. Students receive an A on Friday's spelling test and then misspell many of the same words in their writing on Monday. Teachers are frustrated that their students can't spell. What is the solution? Practice, practice, practice! Teachers want spelling practice to be simple and easy. Students want spelling games that are motivational and fun. Here are 25 games that are fun, easy, and, most important, effective.

The ability to spell well is a sign of literacy. Spelling is a skill of constructing words rather than memorizing them. A good speller predicts how a word is spelled based on knowledge of what is probable in English. Sadly, spelling is one of the most neglected subjects of study. At all grade levels, students benefit from direct instruction and frequent practice in spelling. Spelling instruction is reinforced through activities that:

☆ apply spelling words to daily reading and writing

☆ build phonemic awareness and phonics skills

☆ emphasize basic spelling patterns and generalizations

☆ promote word analysis and build vocabularies

☆ help students correct common spelling errors

☆ stress proofreading skills

☆ develop student interest

A worthwhile spelling program includes the following characteristics:

☆ about 15 minutes of daily instruction, five days a week

☆ lists of spelling words based on spelling patterns or similar structures

☆ use of a pretest-study-test format

☆ a self-corrected test procedure

☆ a word-study strategy that is both visual and auditory

☆ teaching words as whole units, not parts

☆ a focus on words that are developmentally appropriate and appear frequently in students' reading and writing

☆ opportunities to write spelling words in meaningful contexts

☆ an emphasis on teaching how words are spelled rather than on teaching rules

Spelling ability develops in predictable stages, but students may reach these stages at different ages. By the end of first or beginning of second grade, children usually progress from the phonetic spelling stage, in which they match a letter for each sound, to learning orthographic patterns and word roots. Most second through fourth graders are in this transitional spelling stage. At this stage, children understand many of the constraints of sound-letter correspondence and realize that a sound is often comprised of more than one letter. They know that every syllable contains at least one vowel, although they may misplace a vowel when writing. They are aware that some letters are silent. They experiment with basic prefixes, suffixes, and polysyllabic words. They begin to differentiate homophones and recognize compound words as well.

Learning to spell is a perceptual skill; thus, the activities in this book provide visual, auditory, and kinesthetic reinforcement. Since many of the same sounds in English are spelled in different ways, correct spelling requires a clear visual perception of the letter order of each word. Seeing the word while simultaneously hearing or saying it is an effective study strategy. Writing spelling words in meaningful contexts is also helpful.

Immediate reinforcement, specifically self-correction, is essential. In fact, *self-correction is the single greatest factor in learning to spell*. The games in this book require the speller to check and, if necessary, correct his or her spelling attempts.

Enhancing spelling instruction with games sparks student interest. Although games do not involve real-world reading and writing, they serve to focus the players' attention on the structure of words. This, in turn, helps to create visual images of the words, which students will then use as they read and write. Playing games fosters a positive attitude toward spelling, which is critical to improving spelling skills.

How to Use This Book

To learn new spelling words most effectively, students need a systematic approach to studying each word—a word study procedure that is auditory, visual, and kinesthetic. They also need frequent practice to reinforce the concepts, patterns, and rules they're learning about syllabication and word structure. *25 Super-Fun Spelling Games* is a perfect supplement to any spelling program because it provides the reinforcement necessary to place words in long-term memory. In addition, research supports that *motivation* in learning to spell is essential. Since students are enthusiastic about games and group activities, they will be motivated to develop their spelling skills and they'll have fun in the process.

25 Super-Fun Spelling Games is designed for second through fourth graders of all learning styles and can be used independently, in pairs, and in groups. You'll find variations to use with ESL students and with students at different stages of spelling development, as well as suggestions for alternate grouping. For students who need extra support, try using the variations for younger students.

Many of the games in this book involve little or no preparation. Some require no special materials; others require materials that are reproducible or reusable, such as cards or game boards. Laminating materials or mounting them on cardboard will increase their durability. You may also need to provide dice, index cards, writing materials, and playing pieces (plastic chips from other games, dried beans or pasta, buttons, or multicolored paper clips work well).

25 Super-Fun Spelling Games can be used with any spelling list. You can use words from your current classroom spelling program, from a reading or phonics series, or from books of word lists. Word lists, whether organized by spelling pattern, frequency, or developmental level, are highly useful. While it is helpful for students to learn to spell curriculum-related vocabulary, these words are not usually related by pattern. Include such words as a supplement to your weekly list of core words. Second graders can put these "challenge" words on cards in a word bank, while older students can alphabetize them in a file box for handy reference. In the same way, students can keep track of the words they commonly misspell when they write. Once students master the basic sight words, they will be able to spell a high proportion of the words they write. Surprisingly, of the approximately half-million words in the English language, one-third of all our writing is made up of 31 words!

To bridge the gap between school and home, encourage your students to work on their spelling skills with their families. Make extra copies of the game materials so that students can play with friends and family members. This provides an excellent way for families to get involved in your spelling program and for students to gain extra spelling practice.

Word Sorts

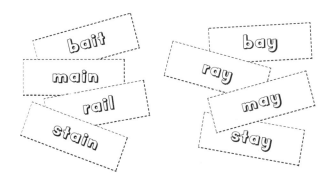

MATERIALS
☆ Word Sort Cards (page 41 or 43)
☆ marker
☆ Word Sort Forms (page 42 or 44), optional
☆ pencils, optional

Word Sort Cards

PREPARATION

Use pages 41–42 for younger students and pages 43–44 for older students.

Write words on cards or have students copy words from a spelling list onto individual cards. Choose two or more spelling patterns to reinforce.

To make the cards reusable, laminate them and use a grease pencil or washable marker.

SUGGESTED GROUPING

individuals

Word sort activities promote fluency and help students become sensitive to recurring patterns and contrasting features within target word groups. At first, have students sort words by categories you specify (closed sorts), such as the long *a* sound, spelled *ai* or *ay*. Once these words can be easily sorted, include words that do not fit into the categories. Later, invite students to sort words by categories of their own choosing (open sorts). Begin with basic word families in grade 2. By grade 4, address how common roots function. This hands-on activity helps students place new spelling words into long-term memory.

PLAY

1. Mix up a set of word cards and give them to the student.

2. Invite the student to read the words and then sort them into two categories that you identify.

3. You may wish to allot time for the student to copy the words in two columns according to the spelling patterns.

Variations

❋ To extend the activity, have students try to sort the words another way, such as by the number of letters in the words or by initial sound. Or encourage students to sort words into categories of their own choosing. Then, on a copy of page 42 or 44, have them write the words in each category in a separate column. They can repeat the activity one or more times to sort the words into two different categories.

❋ Sort the word cards into categories for younger students. Encourage them to look for visual similarities in each category and to read the words aloud to listen for similarities. Ask students to determine how the words in each category are alike.

❋ Ask ESL students to work with non-ESL partners to sort words into two categories. To begin, the non-ESL students can sort the words and the ESL students can identify what is similar about the words in each category. Then partners can work together to sort other words into categories.

Concentration

Attention to visual aspects of words is an important part of spelling. For example, visual discrimination is the ability to differentiate the letter *b* from the letters *d*, *p*, or *h*. For a visual matching game, such as Concentration, it is best to focus on words that students use most in their writing. In addition to visual discrimination, visual memory is important in Concentration. Remembering where words are located enables players to form matches in subsequent turns.

PLAY

1 Mix up the cards and place them face-down in rows of equal number. For example, place 16 cards in 4 rows of 4 cards or 30 cards in 6 rows of 5 cards.

2 Players alternate turning over two cards and reading aloud the words on the cards. If the cards match, the player removes them, keeps them, and takes another turn. If they do not match, the player returns them to their original positions.

3 Play continues until all the matches have been made. The player who has the most cards wins.

Variations

✻ Make pairs of cards with a homophone on each. Then mix up all the cards. The goal is to match homophone pairs. The player who makes a match uses both words in one sentence, if possible, or chooses one of the words to use in a sentence. His or her partner uses the other word in a sentence.

✻ Make pairs of cards with a different form of the same verb on each card. For example, write a present-tense verb on one card (*walk*) and add an inflected ending for the second card (*walked* or *walking*). Then mix up the pairs for players to match.

✻ Have players match:
— consonant blends with phonograms
— comparative/superlative forms of adjectives
— two shorter words in a compound word
— two syllables to make a polysyllabic word

Go Fish for Words

MATERIALS
☆ Go Fish Cards
   (page 45)
☆ marker

PREPARATION
Provide pairs of playing cards for words with a particular sound-letter relationship, such as /ā/ *ai, ay*. (See lists on page 55.)

SUGGESTED GROUPING
partners or groups of 2–4 players

Spelling and word recognition abilities are closely related. Simple card games provide active, hands-on reinforcement of spelling words, and they are especially helpful to students who need extra support. You can reuse the same cards for any of the card games.

Use word pairs to compare and contrast spellings for one sound, such as /ā/ *ai, ay*; particular sound/letter relationships, such as long and short vowels, or base words and words with inflected endings.

PLAY

1 Shuffle the cards.

2 Deal five–eight cards to each player and place the rest facedown in a pile.

3 Players check their hand to see if any pairs exist. If a pair exists, the player reads the word, spells it, and places the pair on the table.

4 Once all of the existing pairs are on the table, the first player asks another player for a card he or she needs to make a match.

5 If the second player has the card, he or she gives it to the first player. That player reads the word, spells it, and places the cards on the table. If the second player does not have the requested card, he or she says "Go fish," and the other player draws a card from the pile. Whenever a player makes a match, he or she takes another turn. Otherwise, the next player takes a turn.

6 The first player to get rid of all his or her cards gets to shuffle, deal, and start the next game.

Variation

❋ Provide blank cards for older students to write their own matching pairs. Specify the sound-letter relationships you wish to reinforce.

Go Fish for Letters

MATERIALS

☆ Go Fish Cards (page 45)
☆ marker
☆ dictionary

PREPARATION

Provide a set of cards with a letter written on each card. Include extra letters for the different spellings of a specific vowel sound you may wish to reinforce. For example, for long *a* words, provide multiple copies of the letters *a, i, y, e,* in addition to consonants that can be used to make words.

SUGGESTED GROUPING

partners or groups of 2–4 players

PLAY

1. Mix up the cards and deal at least five cards to each player. Place the rest facedown in a pile.

2. Players try to make one or more words using the letters in their hand. If a word is formed, they remove the cards, form the word, and read it aloud. If other players disagree about the spelling of the word, they can consult a dictionary. The player who uses all of his or her letters first wins the round.

3. If a player cannot form a word, he or she determines which additional letters are needed to spell a word. The player then asks another player for a specific letter. If that player does not hold the letter, the first player takes the top card from the pile and tries to form a word.

4. Players alternate turns until someone is left with no cards.

Similar Sounds

CAP

CAPE

MATERIALS
☆ Playing Cards (page 46)
☆ marker

PREPARATION
Make pairs of word cards using the word list below.

SUGGESTED GROUPING
partners or groups of 2–4 players

PLAY

1. Deal an equal number of cards to each player.

2. Players check their hands for matching pairs. If players can make any matches, they read aloud the two words, spell them, and place them on the table.

3. The first player selects a card from the player to his or her left. If the card picked matches a card in his or her hand, the player reads aloud the words, spells them, places them on the table, and takes another turn. If not, the next player takes a turn.

4. Players alternate turns until someone is left with no cards.

Word Lists

Use pairs of playing cards to compare or contrast words with similar spellings. For example, choose word pairs with a particular sound-letter relationship, such as /ā/ *ai, ay*; word pairs with a long and short vowel; or base words and words with an inflected ending. Here are some suggestions:

may	may	play	pay	stay	jay	ray	pay	gray	ray	spray	tray
main	maid	plain	paid	stain	jail	rail	pain	grain	rain	sprain	train

cap	pan	plan	tap	hop	cod	can	Sam	man	hat	rip
cape	pane	plane	tape	hope	code	cane	same	mane	hate	ripe

hope	hop	play	skip	eat	race	ride	bake
hoped	hopping	played	skipping	eating	raced	riding	baking

Spelling Bingo

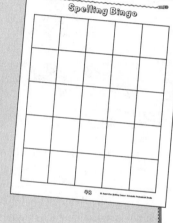

PLAY

1 As you call out each word from the spelling list, students write the word on the bingo board in any box they choose (one word per box).

2 Write the word on the chalkboard for students to check and correct their spelling.

3 When students have filled all the boxes, call out the words again in any order. Check off each word as you call it. Players place a chip on each word as it is read aloud.

4 The first player with a complete row of chips (horizontal, vertical, or diagonal) calls out "Bingo."

5 Confirm the words with the list and ask the player to spell each word in the row.

6 The winner becomes the next caller.

Variations

❋ For ESL students or younger children, provide bingo boards on which the words have already been written. Write the words in a different order on each board. This game will help students recognize words with the same pattern.

❋ For an extra challenge, distribute bingo boards on which letters have been written in the boxes in random order. As you call out letters, players place chips in the corresponding boxes. As soon as the letters in those boxes can be used to form a word containing at least three letters, the player calls out "Bingo" and spells the word he or she formed.

Soccer Spelling

PLAY

1. Have players sit at opposite goals facing each other with the game board between them. Place a set of word cards facedown in each goal.

2. Place the playing pieces on the center line to start the game.

3. The first player reads the top word in the pile in his or her goal.

4. The other player writes the word on the first line heading toward the opponent's goal. Then the player self-checks by looking at the word card. If the word is spelled correctly, the player moves his or her marker on the line with the word. If incorrect, the player corrects the word, returns the card to the bottom of the pile, and does not advance the marker.

5. Players alternate turns until one of them reaches the goal, scoring a point.

6. A player who scores a goal returns his or her playing piece to the center line. Play continues to see who scores more goals. Students can write new words next to previously written words. Once all the word cards in a pile have been spelled, provide additional words or have students mix up the same cards and use them again.

MATERIALS

☆ Soccer Spelling game board (page 14)
☆ 2 playing pieces
☆ pencils and erasers
☆ Word Sort Cards (page 43)

PREPARATION

Make a copy of the game board. You may wish to laminate the board so that students can write on it with markers and reuse it.

Write spelling words on two sets of cards. (You may wish to write each word in a short sentence.)

Mix up each set of cards.

SUGGESTED GROUPING

partners

Variations

❋ Players can spell the words aloud or write the words on paper instead of on the game board, moving their playing pieces down the field each time a word is spelled correctly.

❋ A group of students can play by forming two teams. Players on each team take turns spelling the words. Have them write the words on the chalkboard. Players who spell words correctly move their team's playing piece to the next line, working their way down the field. After a goal is scored, both teams' playing pieces are returned to the center line and play continues.

Soccer Spelling

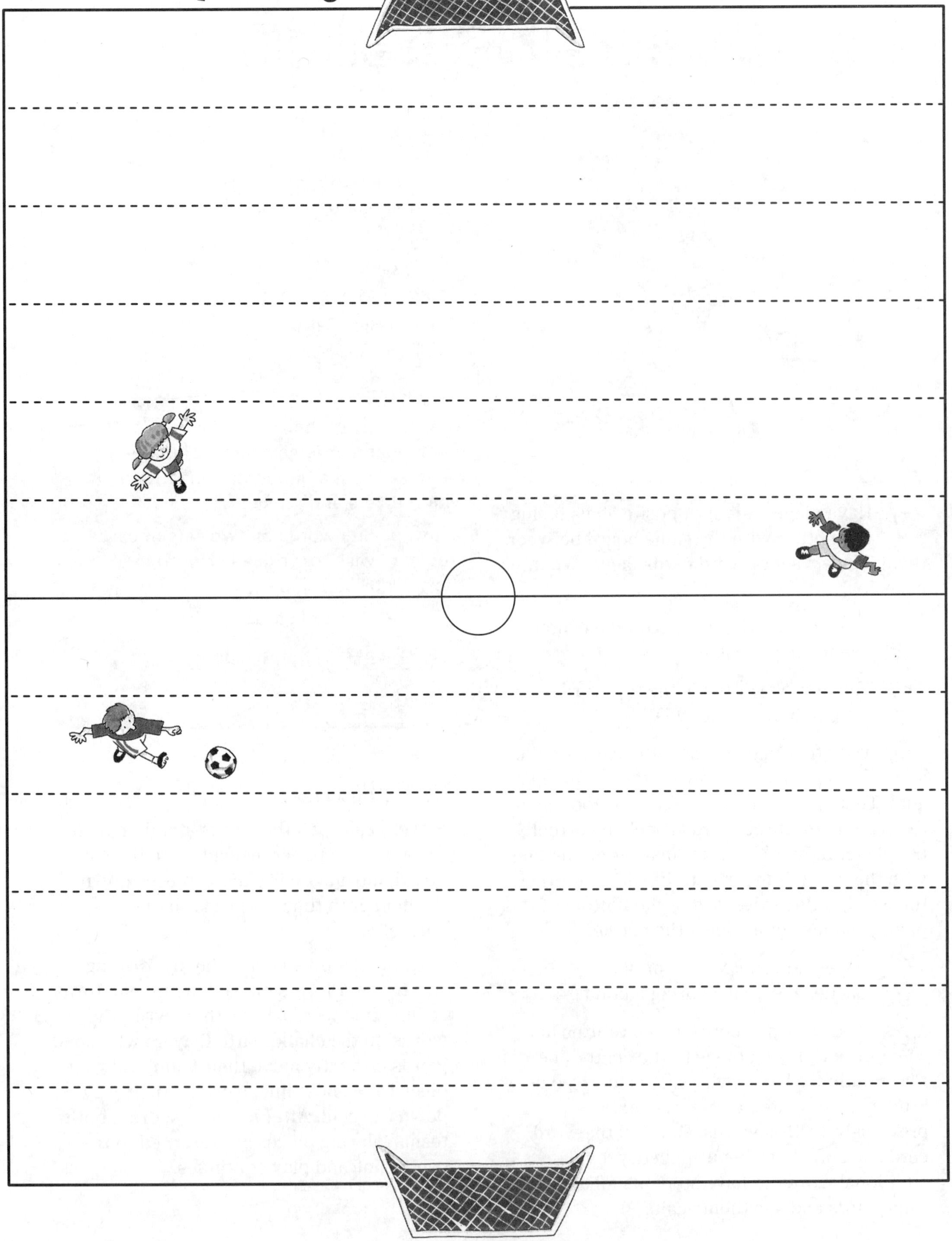

---

25 Super-Fun Spelling Games Scholastic Professional Books

Rock Climb

MATERIALS

☆ Rock Climb game board (page 16)
☆ pencils and erasers
☆ spelling list with 25 numbered words that progress from easy to more difficult
☆ small paper clip

PREPARATION

Make a copy of the game board for each student.

SUGGESTED GROUPING

partners

PLAY

1. Players determine who will be the "climber" and who will be the "caller" for the first round.

2. The climber starts by placing a paper clip on a rock at the bottom of the page (numbers 1–4).

3. The caller reads the numbered word that corresponds to the numbered rock the paper clip is touching. The climber writes the word on the bottom line.

4. The caller writes the word on the chalkboard so that the climber can self-check and if necessary correct his or her own spelling.

5. The climber holds one end of the paper clip on the bottom rock and angles the other end so that touches a higher rock. The caller reads the word, and the climber writes it on the next line. Players then repeat step 4.

6. The climber continues to move to higher rocks in any order. For example, he or she can follow the sequence 2–6–10–14–17–20–24. Play continues for a specified period of time to see if the climber can reach the top (numbers 23, 24, or 25).

7. Players switch roles for the second round.

Rock Climb

25 Super-Fun Spelling Games Scholastic Professional Books

Keep Climbing

MATERIALS

☆ Keep Climbing game board (page 18)
☆ pencils and erasers
☆ list of spelling words that progress from easy to more difficult

PREPARATION

Make a copy of the game board for each student.

SUGGESTED GROUPING

small groups or whole class

PLAY

1 Ask for a volunteer to be the caller and give him or her the word list.

2 The caller reads out each word and uses it in a sentence.

3 As the caller reads the words, the players write them on the lines on their game board, starting at the bottom of the page.

4 After players have written each word, the caller writes the word on the chalkboard so that players can self-check. If incorrect, the players self-correct.

5 When the caller reads the next word, the players write it on the next line or on the same line if the last word was spelled incorrectly.

6 Play continues in this manner until one player reaches the top.

Keep Climbing

25 Super-Fun Spelling Games Scholastic Professional Books

Spelling Space Race

This game provides a fun way to practice spelling words and review different spelling patterns.

PLAY

1. Players place their chips in a pile on Earth.

2. Players take turns "traveling" to a planet of their choice. A partner or designated caller selects a word card from that planet's envelope and reads the word aloud.

3. The player writes the word on the chalkboard and self-checks with the card. If correct, he or she places a chip on the planet to show that the voyage was successful.

4. Repeat the procedure with the other player(s).

5. The game ends when one player has a chip on every planet.

Variation

❋ Play Spelling Space Race with larger groups by dividing children into two teams. Teammates can take turns spelling.

MATERIALS

☆ Spelling Space Race game board (page 20)
☆ Word Sort Cards (page 43)
☆ 8 chips of the same color per player (or small squares of construction paper)
☆ chalkboard and chalk, or clipboard, paper, and pencil
☆ 8 envelopes

PREPARATION

Make one copy of the game board.

Write spelling words on cards. Categorize them by 8 different patterns.

Label each envelope with the name of a planet.

Place one category of cards in each envelope. For fourth graders, for instance, include categories such as words with schwa, *r*-controlled vowels, consonant digraphs, consonant blends, /s/s, c; /j/j, g; /z/z, s; /n/n, kn; /f/f, ph, gh. Include in each envelope one or more cards per player.

SUGGESTED GROUPING

partners or small groups

Spelling Space Race

25 Super-Fun Spelling Games Scholastic Professional Books

Word Roller Coaster

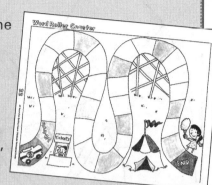

MATERIALS

☆ Word Roller Coaster game board (page 22)

☆ one die

☆ chalkboard and chalk, or clipboard, paper, and pencil

☆ playing pieces

☆ numbered list of 25 spelling words

PREPARATION

Make a copy of the game board.

Number the spaces 1–25 on the game board.

SUGGESTED GROUPING

partners or small groups

PLAY

1 Each player puts a playing piece on START.

2 The first player rolls the die and moves his or her playing piece that number of spaces.

3 When the player lands on a space, the teacher or a caller reads the spelling word on the list that corresponds to the number of the space.

4 The player writes the word on the chalkboard or paper. If spelled incorrectly, the player self-corrects before erasing the chalkboard and then moves his or her playing piece back one space.

5 The first player to reach the end of the ride wins.

Variations

❋ For older students, write one word of a homophone pair in each space. The player reads the word, uses it in a sentence, and spells the other homophone in the pair.

❋ In each space, write a singular noun for which players spell the plural form. Include words in which -s and -es are added, as well as irregular plural forms. Or write verbs that players spell with the inflected ending -ed or -ing. For third and fourth graders, include verbs with final e or those in which the final consonant is doubled.

❋ Write one part of a compound word in each space. Players add another short word to form a compound word, such as racetrack, nighttime, or outside.

Word Roller Coaster

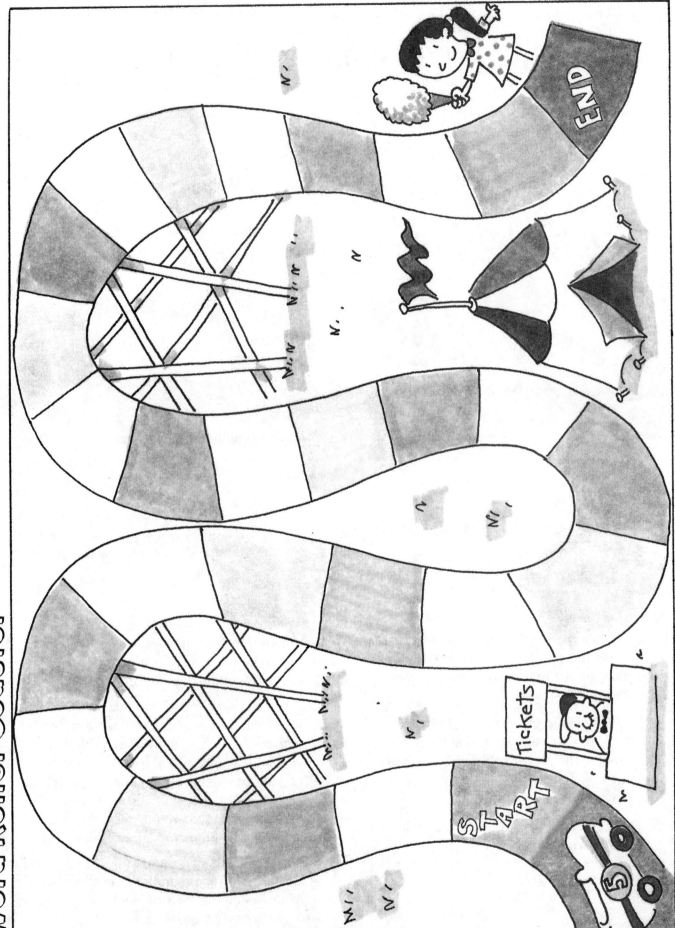

25 Super-Fun Spelling Games Scholastic Professional Books

Archaeological Dig

MATERIALS

☆ Archaeological Dig game board (page 24)

☆ numbered list of 25 words that progress from easy to more difficult

☆ playing pieces

☆ one die

☆ chalkboard and chalk, or clipboard, paper, and pencil

PREPARATION

Make a copy of the game board.

SUGGESTED GROUPING

partners or small groups

PLAY

1 Each player puts a playing piece on START.

2 The first player rolls the die and moves his or her playing piece that number of spaces.

3 When a player lands on a space, the teacher or a caller reads the spelling word on the list that corresponds to the number of the space. If directions appear on the space, the player follows them.

4 The player writes the word on the chalkboard or paper. If spelled incorrectly, the player self-corrects before erasing the chalkboard and then moves his or her playing piece back one space.

5 The first player to reach the end wins.

Archaeological Dig

START	**1**	**2**	Keep digging. Move ahead one.	**3**	Dig some more.
4	Take a rest. Move back one.	**5**	**6**	**7**	You're getting close! Roll again.
Dig, dig, dig.	**8**	You've hit a rock! Move back one.	**9**	Time for lunch. Skip a turn.	**10**
11	Sift some more. Roll again.	**12**	Measure artifacts.	**13**	**14**
Take a rest. Move back two.	**15**	Your shovel breaks. Skip a turn.	**16**	**17**	Get a new shovel. Move ahead two.
18	**19**	**20**	Sifting time. Roll again.	Weigh artifacts.	**21**
22	Photograph artifacts.	**23**	**24**	**25**	FINISH

25 Super-Fun Spelling Games Scholastic Professional Books

Add a Letter

Students can manipulate letter cards, magnetic letters, or letter tiles to build words. This hands-on activity reinforces sound-letter relationships and helps students learn how to look for patterns in words. Using individual sets of several letters to make words, students discover that changing just one letter changes the entire word. In a 10-minute period, students build two- and three-letter words and progress to longer words until they build the final word using all the letters in the set.

PLAY

1. Have players line up their letter cards in alphabetical order.

2. Give players a word to spell using their cards. Start with a two- or three-letter word. Tell players how many letters they need to choose to build the word. Use the word in a sentence.

3. After players have spelled the word, you may wish to use large letter cards in a pocket chart to spell the word. Encourage players to check their word and rearrange the letters if necessary.

MATERIALS

☆ Letter Cards (pages 49–50)

☆ set of larger letter cards and pocket chart, (optional)

PREPARATION

Copy a set of letter cards for each student, or have students make their own cards. Have younger students work with a small group of letters and older students work with more. Make multiple cards for vowels and other letters that may appear more than once in a word. (Laminate the cards for greater durability.)

Determine the final word students will spell using all their letter cards. (A seven-letter word works well.) Consider sound-letter relationships you can point out during the word-building activity, as well as structural analysis, words related to curriculum themes, and student interest.

Then select words, some of which focus on the same pattern. Choose words that your students know. To emphasize the importance of sequence in spelling, try to choose some words that use the same letters.

Write the words on cards or on a list and arrange them from shortest to longest. Also base the order on patterns and similarity of letters.

SUGGESTED GROUPING

individuals or small groups

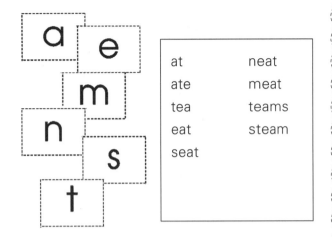

at	neat
ate	meat
tea	teams
eat	steam
seat	

4 Continue to have players build new words. For each new word, tell them how many letters need to be changed or added.

5 Before telling students the final word, ask them to guess what it is. Then tell them the final word to spell.

Variations

✻ For ESL students, place the word card in a pocket chart after they build each word. Reinforce unfamiliar vocabulary by using the word in a sentence pattern several times for students to repeat. For example:

Hamburger is meat. Meat: m-e-a-t.
Pork is meat. Meat: m-e-a-t.
_____ (students provide) is meat.
Meat: m-e-a-t.

✻ For younger students, write a word on the chalkboard. Have students copy the word using their letter cards. Remind them to check their work. Repeat with other words.

✻ Have older students work with a complete alphabet of letter cards to build a word you say. Then challenge them to change one letter at a time to make new words on their own. They can record them on a sheet of paper. You may wish to provide a starting and ending word and the number of changes the players will need to make in order to reach the final word.

✻ Use letter cards to help players "see" how inflected endings are added to verbs. Say a verb such as *hike*, then say it with different endings, such as *hikes*, *hiked*, *hiking*. Players manipulate the letter cards to change the word each time. You may wish to have volunteers take turns suggesting words. Include duplicate consonant letters if any words require doubling the final consonant before adding endings.

Word Ladder

MATERIALS

☆ Word Ladder (page 51)

☆ pencil and erasers

☆ chalkboard and chalk

☆ list of words that can become new words by reordering the letters or by changing or adding one letter

PREPARATION

Make a copy of the word ladder for each student.

SUGGESTED GROUPING

individuals, small groups, or whole class

PLAY

1 Tell students a word to write in the space above the bottom rung of the ladder. Then write it on the chalkboard so that they can check and correct their spelling.

2 Read the next word and have students write it in the space above the next rung. Then write the word on the chalkboard so that they can check and correct their spelling. Continue in this manner until students reach the top of the ladder.

Variations

❋ Invite older students to build new words independently. Indicate the first and last words in a sequence, directing students to change one letter at a time to reach the final word.

❋ For younger students, provide a starting word. For each rung, tell them to change one letter to make a new word you specify. In this way, you can focus on particular sounds or word patterns. For example, for s-blends: *swing, sling, sting, string, strung.*

❋ Record word-building directions on an audiocassette. Students can stop the cassette after each word and write the word on the ladder. Provide an answer key so that students can check their work when they have filled in their ladder.

Word Detective

MATERIALS
☆ Letter Cards (pages 49–50)
☆ list of spelling words

PREPARATION
Copy a set of Letter Cards, making multiple cards for vowels and other letters that appear more than once in a spelling word.

SUGGESTED GROUPING
individuals or small groups

PLAY

1. Use letter cards to build a spelling word, or ask a volunteer to build a word.

2. Have players read the word and then turn around.

3. Remove a letter.

4. Have players turn back around to identify the missing letter and tell where it belongs. A volunteer can replace the letter.

5. You may wish to have each player write a sentence using the word.

Variations

✵ Students can play this game with partners, alternating roles.

✵ Instead of removing a letter when students turn around, scramble the order of the letters. Have each player write the word correctly on a piece of paper. Then ask a volunteer to unscramble the letters. Players can check their answers with the reordered letter cards.

Copycat Words

PLAY

1 Write a spelling word on the chalkboard.

2 Ask students to copy the word onto a strip and check their spelling.

3 Have students say the word and spell it. Invite volunteers to use the word in a sentence.

4 Cover up the word on the chalkboard, and ask students to cut apart each letter.

5 Have them say the word again and visualize how to spell it. Then have them rebuild the word using their letters.

6 Reveal the word on the chalkboard so that students can check their work.

Variations

❉ Prepare longer word strips with vertical lines several inches apart. (The spaces between the lines should be the width of a letter card.) Invite younger students to copy a word from the chalkboard onto a word strip, writing one letter in each space. Then have them use a set of letter cards from pages 49–50 to build the word below the word strip. You can also have them cover each letter on the word strip with a letter card.

| f | r | i | e | n | d |

❉ After younger students copy a word from the chalkboard onto a word strip, have them cut apart the onset from the rime (for example, t...ime, l...ate). Then invite students to say each part of the word as they move the two parts together. Finally, have them join the two parts and say the word.

Copycat Sentences

MATERIALS

☆ sentence strips
☆ pencils and erasers
☆ scissors
☆ chalkboard and chalk

PREPARATION

Make a list of sentences that each include several words with a specific spelling pattern or sound-symbol relationship. For example, "Eat lean meat and beans."

Give a blank sentence strip to each student.

SUGGESTED GROUPING

small groups

Cutting apart words in a sentence reinforces word order, an important concept of print.

PLAY

1. Write a sentence from your list on the chalkboard.

2. For far-point copying practice, students then write the sentence on their sentence strip.

3. Players cut apart the words.

4. Players group words with the same pattern. Encourage them to brainstorm other words with the same pattern.

5. Cover the sentence on the chalkboard and ask students to reassemble the sentence using the word cards.

6. Uncover the sentence so that players can check their work.

7. Repeat the above procedure with other sentences.

Variations

❋ Extend the activity by covering up the sentence after players check their work. Then have them try to write the sentence on the chalkboard from memory. See Look, Say, Write! on page 33.

❋ For younger students, specify the pattern or provide an exemplar for step 4.

❋ For older students, have a volunteer write another sentence on the chalkboard. Encourage the volunteer to use two or more words that have the same pattern as words from the previous sentence. Then repeat steps 2–6.

Word Search

MATERIALS

☆ notebook or Word Sort Forms (page 42 or 44)

☆ pencils

PREPARATION

SUGGESTED GROUPING

individuals or small groups

T his task provides students the opportunity to look for words and write them. This helps them to attend to more abstract patterns of language. It is another way to promote accuracy in recognizing recurring patterns and contrasting features within target word groups. Games such as Concentration and board games on pages 12–23 can be used for further reinforcement of the spelling of the words students find.

PLAY

1 Suggest a spelling pattern for students to look for in words from various sources. They can look in their own writing, in magazines, in books, or on classroom charts, labels, and signs.

2 Provide one or more exemplars illustrating the spelling pattern to get students started, if necessary. Have students copy the words in their notebooks or on their Word Sort Forms.

3 When the word search is over, have small groups of students share their lists to compare common words they located.

Variations

❊ For a quick activity, allow students one minute to record as many words with the same spelling pattern as they can think of. They can look around the room for ideas.

❊ As students share their lists, record all the words on a chart. How many different words did the group come up with? Ask students if they can think of homophones for any of the words. You may prefer to have students search for words at home and record them. Invite students to share their words the next day.

❊ Ask students to search for words with a specific sound that has more than one spelling, such as /j/ spelled *j* or *g*. They can record the words on a Word Sort Form (page 42 or 44). Or have students find words with the *-ed* ending. Then encourage them to sort the words into three groups, according to ending sounds /d/, /t/, or /ed/. The words can then be shared and compared in groups or with the entire class.

Tic-Tac-Toe

PLAY

1 The first player chooses a word card from the bag and reads the word aloud. His or her partner writes the word anywhere on the tic-tac-toe grid and confirms the spelling with the card. Then the second player chooses a card and reads the word, and the first player writes the word on the grid and checks the spelling.

2 Players continue until all spaces on the grid are filled in. Then a player mixes up the cards and places them facedown in a pile.

3 The first player turns over the top card and reads the word.

4 He or she marks X or O on the word.

5 Players take turns doing this.

6 A player wins by getting three marks in a row (vertical, horizontal, or diagonal) and calling out "Tic-Tac-Toe." The winner reads the three words aloud, writes them on the chalkboard or on paper, and takes the first turn in the next game.

7 Let players play three games before replacing the word cards.

MATERIALS
☆ pencil and paper, chalk and chalkboard, or bingo board (page 47)
☆ index cards
☆ bag

Spelling Bingo

47

PREPARATION
Write spelling words on index cards and place them in a bag.

Make a tic-tac-toe grid by drawing two vertical lines intersected by two horizontal lines. Or laminate the grid on page 47 for repeated use.

Have partners decide who will be X and who will be O.

SUGGESTED GROUPING
partners

Variations

❊ Draw a tic-tac-toe grid on the chalkboard, or use masking tape for a more permanent grid. Provide different-colored chalk for each player. Have a student call out the words on the word cards. As the caller reads the word, a player writes the word in a box of his or her choice. Then the player checks the spelling with the word card. A misspelled word is corrected, then erased and rewritten. Players alternate turns until one of them has written three words in a row and calls out "Tic-Tac-Toe."

❊ For an extra challenge, have students correct misspelled words and then erase them. A player who makes no errors has an advantage in this game.

Look, Say, Write!

MATERIALS
☆ sentence strips
☆ marker
☆ pencil, paper, and clipboard

PREPARATION
On sentence strips, write short, meaningful sentences. Use words with familiar patterns that students are attempting to master, as well as sight words.

Progress to longer sentences.

Coach students to use this strategy when trying to increase visual memory: Look at the sentence (focusing on the number of words), read it, say it to yourselves, and picture the words before you write them.

Depending on ability, start younger students with two- and three-word phrases or sentences.

SUGGESTED GROUPING
individuals or small groups

Students build visual/kinesthetic memory by first looking at a phrase or short sentence and then trying to write it from memory. When they have finished writing, students self-correct by looking back at the phrase or sentence.

PLAY

1. Display a sentence strip for approximately five seconds. (You can vary the time according to students' needs.)

2. Students then turn around and write the sentence or phrase that was displayed.

3. Have students check what they wrote before they confirm their work with the sentence strip.

4. Repeat with other sentences.

Variations

* Dictate phrases or short sentences. Remind students to listen carefully and to repeat to themselves what they heard. Then have students write and proofread their work. Read the phrase or sentence aloud a second time for them to check their work. Write the phrase or sentence on the chalkboard and allow students to make any necessary spelling corrections.

* You may wish to tape-record sentences for students to work independently.

Cool Crosswords

MATERIALS

☆ Crossword Grid (page 52)

☆ pencils and erasers

PREPARATION

Make a copy of the Crossword Grid for each student.

Write a list of spelling words on chart paper or on the chalkboard.

Display a simple crossword puzzle (or a Scrabble™ game board with pieces) to demonstrate how a crossword puzzle is completed, if necessary.

SUGGESTED GROUPING

individuals

PLAY

1. Have students select two spelling words that share at least one letter in common.

2. Students determine how to "cross" the words by writing one horizontally on the grid and the other vertically, so that the words share a letter where they intersect.

3. Encourage students to add other spelling words to their grid.

Variations

❋ Have younger students use the bingo board instead (page 47 or 48). Some students may find it easier to manipulate Letter Cards (pages 49–50) or letter tiles rather than use paper and pencil. Suggest that they repeat the task with other pairs of words. When they are comfortable with this, encourage students to add a third word to each pair of words they have crossed.

❋ For an extra challenge, suggest that students cross words to create a puzzle. Have them number each box containing the first letter of a word. On a separate sheet of paper they can write a clue for each word, organizing them into "across" and "down" categories. Suggest that they use brief definitions, synonyms, antonyms, or fill-in-the-blank sentences for their clues. Finally, have students outline the boxes for their puzzle and copy the outline and numbers onto a blank crossword grid. Partners exchange crossword grids and clues and complete each other's puzzles. They can check their work with their partner's original crossword grid.

Pass the Pad

MATERIALS
☆ pad of paper and pencil
☆ paper bag
☆ audiocassette player and recorded music
☆ index cards
☆ marker

PREPARATION
Write spelling words on cards, or have children write the words. Place word cards in a paper bag.

SUGGESTED GROUPING
small groups

PLAY

1 Invite students to sit in a circle. Play music while students pass the paper and pencil around the circle.

2 Periodically stop the music and choose a word from the bag. Read the word aloud.

3 The player who is holding the pad when the music stops writes the word you read.

4 The player displays the word and confirms its spelling with the card. If the word is spelled correctly, he or she remains in the circle. If not, the player corrects the spelling and comes out of the circle. He or she reads the spelling word the next time the music stops.

5 Continue playing until all the words have been spelled or just one player remains in the circle.

Variation

❋ Pass a pad and pencil around the circle as the music plays. When the music stops, the player holding the pad writes a letter. Continue to pass the pad around the circle until the music stops again. The player holding the pad adds another letter to build a spelling word. Subsequent players try to add letters to complete a word. Confirm the spelling of the completed word with the group. With a new sheet of paper, begin again.

Word Chains

MATERIALS
- ☆ multicolored construction paper cut into 7- by 1-inch strips
- ☆ markers
- ☆ paste or tape
- ☆ student word banks or spelling lists

PREPARATION

SUGGESTED GROUPING

partners

PLAY

1. One student selects a word from a word bank or spelling list and writes the word on a strip.

2. The other student thinks of another word that begins with the last letter of the word selected. Students can also use a word from the word bank or spelling list. He or she writes the word on another strip and places it below the first word on a table.

3. Players continue in this manner for a specified period of time.

4. Students then paste or tape together the ends of the first strip, so that the word shows on the outside of the circle. Show them how to make a chain by sliding the next strip through the circle and pasting the ends together. Continue adding word strips to form a long chain.

5. Invite partners to read in unison the words on their chain. To display the chains, thread a string through them and then hang the string like a clothesline.

Variations

☀ Each pair of students can paste their word strips on descending steps drawn on craft paper taped to a wall.

☀ Partners or small groups can make a long line of words by pinning word strips from left to right across a bulletin board. Which group has the longest line?

Give Me a Clue

MATERIALS
☆ index cards
☆ marker
☆ chalkboard and chalk

PREPARATION
Write spelling words on index cards.

SUGGESTED GROUPING
small groups or whole class

Variations

❋ Younger students can write their word on the chalkboard with blanks in place of some letters. After a student has provided one clue about the word, a volunteer guesses the word by filling in the missing letters. The spelling is confirmed with the word card. If correct, that volunteer repeats the procedure by writing his or her word on the chalkboard with some missing letters. If incorrect, students continue guessing.

❋ To play "Kiki the Cat," one student draws blanks on the chalkboard to represent the number of letters in a spelling word. Players take turns guessing letters. If a guessed letter is in the word, the student fills in the corresponding blank with the letter. If the letter is not in the word, the student writes the letter above the word and draws one part of a cat, such as an eye, ear, nose, or outline of the face. When a student wants to guess the word, he or she calls out, "Kiki the Cat." If correct, the student fills in the missing letters. If incorrect, another part of the cat is drawn and play continues. The goal is to guess the word before the picture of the cat is completed.

PLAY

1. Provide each student with a spelling word written on an index card. Ask students to look at their word without telling anyone what it is.

2. Have a volunteer respond to questions about his or her word, such as:

   What is the first sound?

   How many syllables are in the word?

   How many letters are in the word?

3. Ask a second volunteer to guess the word and write it on the chalkboard. Have the same student check his or her spelling with the card. If the student guesses the correct word, he or she can respond to questions next. If the student's guess is incorrect, continue asking questions.

It's a Wonderful Word!

MATERIALS
- ☆ 4- by 6-inch index cards, preferably lined on one side
- ☆ markers
- ☆ chart paper

PREPARATION
none

SUGGESTED GROUPING
small groups

This quick activity will help children expand their vocabularies and learn to spell words that are useful in their writing.

PLAY

1 Give each student an index card. He or she chooses a word and writes it on the lined side of the card. Then the student writes a definition, a synonym or antonym, and a sentence using the word. On the blank side of the card, he or she draws an image to illustrate the word.

2 When students have finished making their "Wonderful Word" cards, have one student show his or her picture to the other members of the group.

3 The group members have three tries to guess the Wonderful Word.

4 Once the word is correctly identified, students take turns to see who can spell the word correctly on a chart of Wonderful Words. If no one correctly spells the word, the student who made the word card writes the word.

5 Students can also take turns using the word in a sentence.

6 Continue until everyone has shared his or her word card.

Variations

✵ When students are finished playing, have each group compose a collaborative story using all the words on the chart. Students may wish to use a computer to compose a round-robin story. Have them take turns adding one or two sentences that include words from the chart.

✵ For spelling reinforcement, have students copy and alphabetize the words on the chart.

Write, Write, Write: Ways to Write Words Creatively

According to current research, students learn to spell words by writing them repeatedly in a meaningful context. Provide students with frequent opportunities to write new or difficult spelling words. For example, have them use the same spelling words in a story, in a poem, and on a poster. Invite students to use colored markers to emphasize the spelling words. This kind of reinforcement helps to fix the visual images of the words in students' minds.

Student motivation is a key element in improved spelling. Provide a variety of tactile and kinesthetic ways for students to write spelling words. Here are some suggestions.

Have students write their spelling words:

❋ in shaving cream or pudding on a table top

❋ in a tray of sand

❋ on the chalkboard with a finger or paintbrush dipped in water

❋ on a partner's hand or back using fingers (then the partner can guess the word)

❋ on their other hand or leg using a finger

❋ with white glue; then have students sprinkle sand or glitter on top

❋ on the computer using an interesting font

❋ with different-colored markers or crayons traced over the word multiple times

❋ using a magic slate

❋ using letter cards, magnetic letters, or letter tiles

❋ using stencils or outlining bulletin board letters

❋ using letters cut out from magazines, newspapers, or cereal boxes

❋ with letter beads strung together

❋ with pipe cleaners or yarn glued onto a piece of cardboard

Have students practice writing their spelling words on a three-column list. Use page 53 for younger students and page 54 for older students. Students write a spelling word in column 1 and copy it in column 2. Then they fold on the dotted line and write the word from memory in column 3. Students unfold the paper to self-check.

Variations

❋ Provide younger students with the words written in column 1 for them to trace.

❋ For an extra challenge, have a student write the spelling words in column 1. In column 2, the student writes a word with the same beginning sound, a word that rhymes, or the plural form. In column 3, the student writes a word with the same spelling pattern, the same number of letters, or the same number of syllables. Encourage students to respond with another word from the spelling list as often as possible.

Word Study Strategy

Look
at the word and the letters in the word.

Read
the word.

Say
the word to yourself.

Picture
the word in your mind.

Write
the word as you remember seeing it.

Check
the word.

You may wish to enlarge this on a photocopier and display it, or make a copy for each student.

Word Sort Cards

Word Sort Form

25 Super-Fun Spelling Games Scholastic Professional Books

Word Sort Cards

Word Sort Form

1. _____
2. _____
3. _____
4. _____
5. _____
6. _____
7. _____
8. _____
9. _____
10. _____

1. _____
2. _____
3. _____
4. _____
5. _____
6. _____
7. _____
8. _____
9. _____
10. _____

1. _____
2. _____
3. _____
4. _____
5. _____
6. _____
7. _____
8. _____
9. _____
10. _____

1. _____
2. _____
3. _____
4. _____
5. _____
6. _____
7. _____
8. _____
9. _____
10. _____

25 Super-Fun Spelling Games Scholastic Professional Books

Go Fish Cards

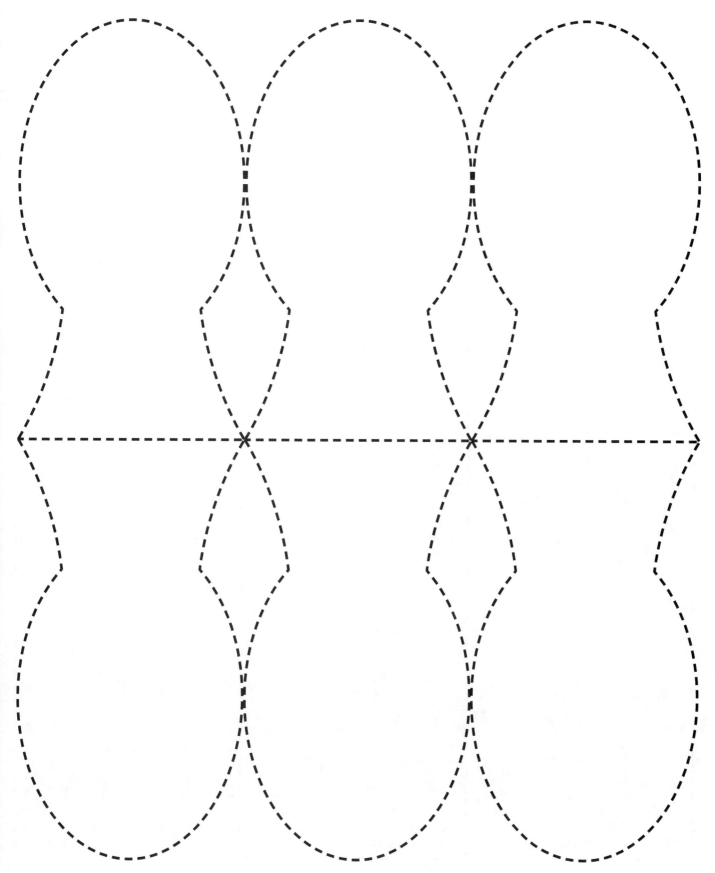

Playing Cards

25 Super-Fun Spelling Games Scholastic Professional Books

Spelling Bingo

Spelling Bingo

25 Super-Fun Spelling Games Scholastic Professional Books

Letter Cards

a	b	c
d	e	f
g	h	i
j	k	l
	m	

Letter Cards

n	o	p
q	r	s
t	u	v
w	x	y
	z	

25 Super-Fun Spelling Games Scholastic Professional Books

Word Ladder

Crossword Grid

25 Super-Fun Spelling Games Scholastic Professional Books

Spelling Practice Sheet

Write a word.	Copy it.	Fold and write.

Spelling Practice Sheet

 25 Super-Fun Spelling Games Scholastic Professional Books

Sample Spelling Words

Short Vowel Sounds

Use two sounds, such as /e/ and /i/, for students to contrast. To review sound-letter relationships, contrast three or more sounds.

/a/   back, cat, chat, dad, fan, grab, hand, jacks, lab, man, nap, ran

/e/   bed, den, hen, lend, men, net, pet, red, sent, shed, ten, vent

/i/   bit, chip, dim, fit, grim, him, kit, lint, miss, rip, skin, spin, wish

/o/   clock, drop, fox, got, hop, job, lock, not, odd, pop, rock

/u/   bug, cut, dug, fun, fuss, hug, jump, lug, nut, rub, sun, tug

Long Vowel Sounds

Provide sets of cards to focus on sound/spellings, such as /ā/ *ai, ay*; /ō/ *oa, ow*; /ī/ *igh, y*. You may wish to include words with the same pattern or you may wish to contrast words with long vowels spelled vowel-consonant-*e*.

/ā/   brain, fail, gain, grain, main, pain, raid, train
bay, clay, day, hay, may, okay, pay, ray, say, way

/ō/   boat, coat, float, goat, load, moan, road, toast
bow, blow, crow, grow, know, low, mow, slow
go, no, so

/ē/   green, keep, see, sheep, three, tree, wheel
beat, cheap, cream, dream, lean, steam, teach, team

Consonant Blends

Make separate games using words with *l*-blends, *r*-blends, and *s*-blends before combining them into one game.

l-blends   black, clay, flap, flake, glad, plate, slam, sling

r-blends   brake, crab, drink, frog, gray, price, print, trip

s-blends   skip, sled, slice, smell, snail, spin, stick, stuff

Consonant Digraphs

Make separate games for words with each digraph before combining them.

/ch/   chain, cheap, check, cheese, chin, chip, chop, chunk

/sh/   shade, shape, shark, shine, ship, shock, shop, short

/hw/   whale, what, wheat, wheel, when, whip, while, white

From ↗

Inflected Endings

Use pairs of word cards for a verb with the *-ed* ending and the same verb with the *-ing* ending. You may also wish to include present-tense verbs + *-ed* and irregular past tenses.

> bike, biking; cook, cooked; jump, jumped; sing, singing;
> write, wrote; run, ran; see, saw; sing, sang

Irregular Plurals

> child, children; goose, geese; mouse, mice; woman, women

Root Words

Make pairs of word cards that have the same root word, such as *unripe* and *ripened*. Students ask other players for word cards with the same root as a card they are holding.

> finish, unfinished; happy, happiness; travel, traveler; wonder, wonderful

Homophones

bare, bear	fair, fare	meat, meet	sew, so
beat, beet	for, four	one, won	some, sum
berry, bury	hair, hare	pail, pale	stare, stair
blew, blue	hall, haul	pair, pear	tail, tale
brake, break	hear, here	plain, plane	threw, through
cell, sell	hour, our	role, roll	to, two, too
cent, sent	know, no	sail, sale	wear, where
dear, deer	mail, male	scene, seen	weather, whether
dew, due	main, mane	sea, see	wood, would

Most Frequently Written Words

If students can recognize and spell the most commonly used words in the English language, their ability to read and write will greatly improve. Twenty-two of the first 25 words make up close to one-third of all written material. The first 100 comprise about half of all printed material. Words are listed in order of their frequency of use.

1. the	10. it	19. they	28. had
2. of	11. he	20. I	29. by
3. and	12. was	21. at	30. word
4. a	13. for	22. be	31. but
5. to	14. on	23. this	32. not
6. in	15. are	24. have	33. what
7. is	16. as	25. from	34. all
8. you	17. with	26. or	35. were
9. that	18. his	27. one	36. we

37. when
38. your
39. can
40. said
41. there
42. use
43. an
44. each
45. which
46. she
47. do
48. how
49. their
50. if
51. will
52. up
53. other
54. about
55. out
56. many
57. then
58. them
59. these
60. so
61. some
62. her
63. would
64. make
65. like
66. him
67. into
68. time
69. has
70. look
71. two
72. more
73. write
74. go
75. see
76. number
77. no

78. way
79. could
80. people
81. my
82. than
83. first
84. water
85. been
86. call
87. who
88. oil
89. its
90. now
91. find
92. long
93. down
94. day
95. did
96. get
97. come
98. made
99. may
100. part
101. over
102. new
103. sound
104. take
105. only
106. little
107. work
108. know
109. place
110. year
111. live
112. me
113. back
114. give
115. most
116. very
117. after
118. thing

119. our
120. just
121. name
122. good
123. sentence
124. man
125. think
126. say
127. great
128. where
129. help
130. through
131. much
132. before
133. line
134. right
135. too
136. mean
137. old
138. any
139. same
140. tell
141. boy
142. follow
143. came
144. want
145. show
146. also
147. around
148. form
149. three
150. small
151. set
152. put
153. end
154. does
155. another
156. well
157. large
158. must
159. big

160. even
161. such
162. because
163. turn
164. here
165. why
166. ask
167. went
168. men
169. read
170. need
171. land
172. different
173. home
174. us
175. move
176. try
177. kind
178. hand
179. picture
180. again
181. change
182. off
183. play
184. spell
185. air
186. away
187. animal
188. house
189. point
190. page
191. letter
192. mother
193. answer
194. found
195. study
196. still
197. learn
198. should
199. America
200. world

From Spelling Book *by Edward Fry. Laguna Beach, California: Laguna Beach Educational Books, 1992.*

Most Commonly Misspelled Words

These 100 words are most commonly misspelled across all grade levels.

1. too	26. didn't	51. like	76. about
2. a lot	27. people	52. whole	77. first
3. because	28. until	53. another	78. happened
4. there	29. with	54. believe	79. Mom
5. their	30. different	55. I'm	80. especially
6. that's	31. outside	56. thought	81. school
7. they	32. we're	57. let's	82. getting
8. it's	33. through	58. before	83. started
9. when	34. upon	59. beautiful	84. was
10. favorite	35. probably	60. everything	85. which
11. went	36. don't	61. very	86. stopped
12. Christmas	37. sometimes	62. into	87. two
13. were	38. off	63. caught	88. Dad
14. our	39. everybody	64. one	89. took
15. they're	40. hear	65. Easter	90. friend's
16. said	41. always	66. what	91. presents
17. know	42. I	67. there's	92. are
18. you're	43. something	68. little	93. morning
19. friend	44. would	69. doesn't	94. could
20. friends	45. want	70. usually	95. around
21. really	46. and	71. clothes	96. buy
22. finally	47. Halloween	72. scared	97. maybe
23. where	48. house	73. everyone	98. family
24. again	49. once	74. have	99. pretty
25. then	50. to	75. swimming	100. tried

25 Super-Fun Spelling Games Scholastic Professional Books

Sample Standardized Test-Taking Practice—Grade 2

Read the words on each line.
Look at how each is spelled.
Color in the circle next to the word that is spelled correctly.

SAMPLE	○ kan	● can	○ cann	○ canne
1.	○ tat	○ taht	○ that	○ thate
2.	○ his	○ hiz	○ hisse	○ hes
3.	○ bt	○ bot	○ bute	○ but
4.	○ mun	○ men	○ menn	○ mans
5.	○ not	○ nott	○ nat	○ nt
6.	○ uv	○ ov	○ uf	○ of
7.	○ wiht	○ weth	○ with	○ wih
8.	○ she	○ shee	○ shi	○ se
9.	○ wut	○ wot	○ whut	○ what
10.	○ eatch	○ each	○ eech	○ eash
11.	○ plase	○ plas	○ place	○ plaise
12.	○ da	○ dey	○ dae	○ day
13.	○ meny	○ manny	○ many	○ mene
14.	○ call	○ cawl	○ caul	○ ca
15.	○ liek	○ licke	○ lik	○ lick
16.	○ know	○ kno	○ kow	○ knoe
17.	○ true	○ trew	○ tru	○ truw
18.	○ wuold	○ wold	○ wuld	○ would
19.	○ goode	○ gud	○ good	○ goud
20.	○ wishs	○ wishes	○ wihses	○ wiches

Sample Standardized Test-Taking Practice—Grade 3

Read the four words on each line. Look at how each word is spelled. Color in the circle next to the word that is spelled correctly.

SAMPLE	○ tat	○ taht	● that	○ thate
1.	○ cresh	○ craish	○ crach	○ crash
2.	○ clok	○ clock	○ cloc	○ clouck
3.	○ teach	○ teech	○ teatch	○ teash
4.	○ mes	○ messe	○ mess	○ mesz
5.	○ thay	○ they	○ thaiy	○ thaye
6.	○ sharm	○ charme	○ chorm	○ charm
7.	○ page	○ pag	○ paje	○ padge
8.	○ traped	○ trappd	○ trapped	○ trapt
9.	○ paintd	○ painted	○ paynted	○ pianted
10.	○ friend	○ freind	○ frend	○ frind
11.	○ baddle	○ batle	○ battel	○ battle
12.	○ esy	○ easy	○ eazy	○ easey
13.	○ drizle	○ drizzel	○ drizel	○ drizzle
14.	○ night	○ nit	○ nite	○ nigte
15.	○ craul	○ crall	○ crawl	○ krawl
16.	○ skool	○ school	○ schol	○ scool
17.	○ senter	○ centr	○ center	○ sentter
18.	○ lissen	○ lisen	○ lisson	○ listen
19.	○ evrything	○ everyting	○ everything	○ every thing
20.	○ babies	○ babys	○ babbies	○ babyes

 25 Super-Fun Spelling Games Scholastic Professional Books

Sample Standardized Test-Taking Practice—Grade 4

Read the four words on each line. Fill in the circle next to the word that is spelled correctly.

SAMPLE ○ boxs ○ boxxes ● boxes ○ bockes

1. ○ pease ○ peice ○ peace ○ piese
2. ○ reade ○ ready ○ redy ○ reddy
3. ○ around ○ arownd ○ aruond ○ arround
4. ○ enouf ○ enugh ○ enouff ○ enough
5. ○ freeze ○ freze ○ freese ○ freez
6. ○ clime ○ climb ○ climbe ○ clim
7. ○ littel ○ litle ○ litel ○ little
8. ○ chaptor ○ chaptar ○ chapter ○ chaptr
9. ○ picture ○ pictore ○ pichture ○ picchure
10. ○ reasin ○ reason ○ reasen ○ reson
11. ○ nattion ○ nashen ○ nashun ○ nation
12. ○ siting ○ sittng ○ sitting ○ sitin
13. ○ sillyest ○ silliest ○ siliest ○ sillist
14. ○ leaves ○ leafs ○ leafes ○ leeves
15. ○ reveiw ○ revewe ○ review ○ revu
16. ○ angery ○ angry ○ angrey ○ angray
17. ○ desagree ○ dissagree ○ diagree ○ disagree
18. ○ quickly ○ quikly ○ qickly ○ quckly
19. ○ forgoten ○ forgotten ○ forgottin ○ forgotton
20. ○ sleeped ○ slepped ○ slept ○ sleped

GAME SIGN-OUT SHEET

GAME	YOUR NAME	DATE	TIME OUT	TIME IN
Spelling Bingo				
Soccer Spelling				
Rock Climb				
Keep Climbing				
Spelling Space Race				
Word Roller Coaster				
Archaeological Dig				

25 Super-Fun Spelling Games Scholastic Professional Books

Professional Bibliography

Adams, Marilyn Jager. *Beginning to Read: Thinking and Learning About Print.* Cambridge, Massachusetts: The MIT Press, 1995.

Barbe, Walter B., Azalia S. Francis, Lois A. Braun. *Basic Skills for Effective Communication.* Columbus: Zaner-Bloser, Inc. 1982.

Blevins, Wiley. *Phonics From A to Z.* New York: Scholastic Professional Books, 1998.

Cunningham, Patricia and James. *The Reading Teacher*, Vol. 46, No. 2, "Making Words: Enhancing the Invented Spelling–Decoding Connection." 1994.

Flood, James, Julie M. Jenson, Diane Lapp, James R. Squire. *Handbook of Research on Teaching the English Language Arts*, Chapter 36. New York: Macmillan, 1991.

Fresch, Mary Jo and Aileen Wheaton. *The Reading Teacher*, Vol. 51, No. 1, "Sort, Search, and Discover: Spelling in the Child-Centered Classroom." September 1997.

Fry, Edward Bernard, Jacqueline E. Kress, and Dona Lee Fountoukidis. *The Reading Teacher's Book of Lists.* Englewood Cliffs, New Jersey: Prentice Hall, 1993.

Graham, Steve. *The Elementary School Journal*, Vol. 81, No. 5, "Effective Spelling Instruction." May 1983.

Graham, Steve and Karen R. Harris. *Journal of Educational Research*, Vol. 86, No. 6, "The Basic Spelling Vocabulary List." pp. 363-368 July/August 1994.

Graves, Donald. *A Fresh Look at Writing.* Portsmouth, New Hampshire: Heinemann, 1994.

Honig, Bill. *Teaching Our Children to Read.* Thousand Oaks, California: Corwin Press, Inc., 1996.

Horn, T. D. "Spelling." *Encyclopedia of Educational Research.* 4th ed. New York: Macmillan, 1969.

Loomer, Bradley M. *Useful Spelling.* Mt. Vernon, Iowa: Useful Learning, 1990.

Moats, Louisa Cook. *Spelling: Development, Disabilities, and Instruction.* Baltimore: York Press, Inc., 1995.

Putnam, Lillian R. *How to Become a Better Reading Teacher: Strategies for Assessment and Intervention.* Paramus, New Jersey: Prentice Hall, 1995.

Schlagel, Robert C. and Joy Harris Schlagal. *Language Arts*, Vol. 69, "The Integral Character of Spelling: Teaching Strategies for Multiple Purposes." October, 1992.

Venezky, Richard L. *Spelling in the Content Areas.* New York: Random House, Inc., 1989.

Notes

25 Super-Fun Spelling Games Scholastic Professional Books